Stellar Space
Space Pioneers

by Julie Murray

Dash!
LEVELED READERS
An Imprint of Abdo Zoom • abdobooks.com

Dash!
LEVELED READERS

Level 1 – Beginning
Short and simple sentences with familiar words or patterns for children who are beginning to understand how letters and sounds go together.

Level 2 – Emerging
Longer words and sentences with more complex language patterns for readers who are practicing common words and letter sounds.

Level 3 – Transitional
More developed language and vocabulary for readers who are becoming more independent.

abdobooks.com

Published by Abdo Zoom, a division of ABDO, PO Box 398166, Minneapolis, Minnesota 55439. Copyright © 2022 by Abdo Consulting Group, Inc. International copyrights reserved in all countries. No part of this book may be reproduced in any form without written permission from the publisher. Dash!™ is a trademark and logo of Abdo Zoom.

Printed in the United States of America, North Mankato, Minnesota.
052021
092021

Photo Credits: Alamy, iStock, NASA
Production Contributors: Kenny Abdo, Jennie Forsberg, Grace Hansen, John Hansen
Design Contributors: Candice Keimig, Neil Klinepier, Victoria Bates

Library of Congress Control Number: 2020919490

Publisher's Cataloging in Publication Data

Names: Murray, Julie, author.
Title: Space pioneers / by Julie Murray
Description: Minneapolis, Minnesota : Abdo Zoom, 2022 | Series: Stellar space | Includes online resources and index.
Identifiers: ISBN 9781098226282 (lib. bdg.) | ISBN 9781098226428 (ebook) | ISBN 9781098226497 (Read-to-Me ebook)
Subjects: LCSH: Outer space--Juvenile literature. | Outer space--Exploration--Juvenile literature. | Manned space flight--History--Juvenile literature. | Astronautics--Juvenile literature. | Orbital transfer (Space flight)--Juvenile literature.
Classification: DDC 629.45009--dc23

Table of Contents

Groundwork 4

Early Astronauts 8

Women in Space 16

More Space Pioneers 22

Glossary 23

Index 24

Online Resources 24

Groundwork

Some space **pioneers** solved math problems or designed rockets so humans could go to space. Others rode aboard those machines. Humans who lived hundreds of years before space flight, like Isaac Newton, are space pioneers too. Newton founded the basic laws of motion and **gravity**.

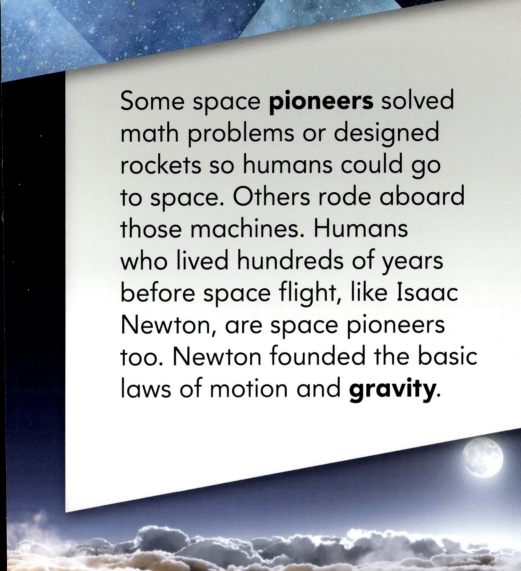

Robert Goddard is called "the father of modern rocketry." He designed, built, and flew rockets. He launched the first liquid-fueled rocket in 1926. His rocket technology is still used for space flight today.

Early Astronauts

On April 12, 1961, Yuri Gagarin, a Russian astronaut, became the first person to go to space and **orbit** Earth. At launch time aboard Vostok 1, Gagarin said, "Off we go!"

Alan Shepard was the first American in space. He rode aboard Freedom 7 on May 5, 1961. The mission went 116 miles (187 km) up in space. It lasted about 15 minutes. Later, in 1971, Shepard would also walk on the moon!

John Glenn was the first American to **orbit** Earth. He did this on February 20, 1962 aboard Friendship 7. In 1998, he became the oldest person to go into space at age 77!

The Apollo 11 mission to the moon was historic! Michael Collins was the command pilot. Neil Armstrong and Buzz Aldrin became the first people to walk on the moon on July 20, 1969.

Women in Space

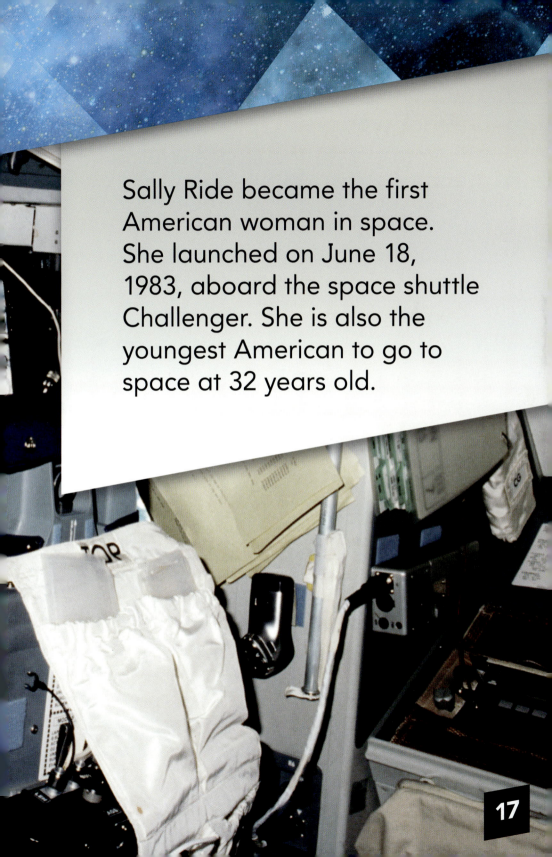

Sally Ride became the first American woman in space. She launched on June 18, 1983, aboard the space shuttle Challenger. She is also the youngest American to go to space at 32 years old.

Mae Jemison was the first Black woman in space. She went up with the space shuttle Endeavor. It took off on September 12, 1992. Jemison spent eight days in space researching and **conducting** experiments.

In 2008, Peggy Whitson became the first woman to command the **International Space Station**. She also holds the US record for most days spent in space at 665.

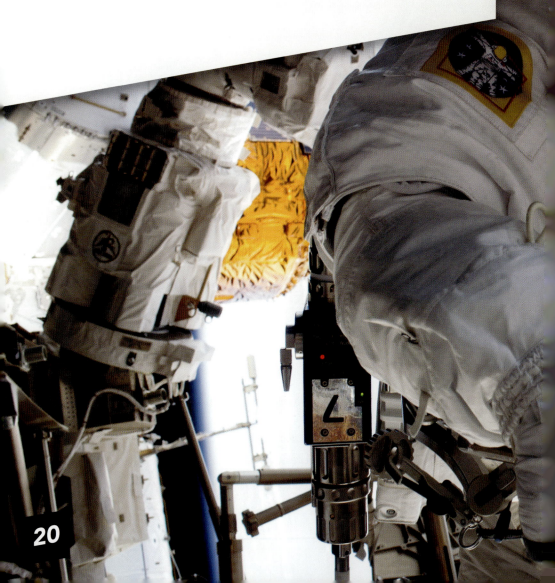

More Space Pioneers

- **Johannes Kepler** – calculated how planets and satellites orbit

- **Valentina Tereshkova** – the first woman to go into space

- **Alexei Leonov** – the first person to walk in space

- **Ed White** – the first American to take a spacewalk

- **Katherine Johnson** – performed important math calculations at NASA for safe space flight

- **Scott Kelly** – spent almost a year in space to study its effects on the human body

Glossary

conducting – leading or managing.

gravity – the force by which all objects in the universe are attracted to each other.

International Space Station (ISS) – a large spacecraft in orbit around Earth. It serves as a home and science laboratory where crews of astronauts live and work. Several nations worked together to build it.

orbit – (n) the curved path in which a natural or artificial body moves in a circle around a star, planet, or moon. (v) to move in a circle around.

pioneer – someone who is one of the first in a culture to do something or explore a place.

Index

Aldrin, Buzz 14
Apollo 11 (mission) 14
Armstrong, Neil 14
Collins, Michael 14
Gagarin, Yuri 8
Glenn, John 12
Goddard, Robert 6
International Space Station 20
Jemison, Mae 18
moon 11, 14
Newton, Isaac 5
Ride, Sally 17
Russia 8
Shepard, Alan 11
Whitson, Peggy 20

Online Resources

To learn more about space pioneers, please visit **abdobooklinks.com** or scan this QR code. These links are routinely monitored and updated to provide the most current information available.